T0160520

Taming the Beast

Managing Anger in Ourselves and Our Children Through Divorce

Benjamin D. Garber, PhD

ISBN 9781936268269 eISBN 9781950057016

Copyright © 2018 by Benjamin D. Garber

Unhooked Books, LLC 7701 E. Indian School Rd., Ste. F Scottsdale, AZ 85251 www.unhookedbooks.com

Library of Congress Control Number: 201853501

Book design: Julian Leon, The Missive
Printed in the United States of America

CONTENTS

Read this First

Anger happens

Anger is as natural and necessary a part of human existence as happiness, sadness and fear

Managed correctly, anger can motivate dramatic change. It can turn a failure into a success, a handicap into a strength and a foe into a friend.

Managed incorrectly, anger can be seen at the root of some of the most traumatic, destructive and violent acts that surround us every day.

Inappropriate expressions of anger hinder success, alienate loved ones, destroy valuables, maim and injure and kill.

As powerful and universal as anger is, few people take the time to understand and nurture healthy expressions of anger until it's too late.

It's not enough to tell a child what NOT to do when he's angry. It's not enough to wait for the crisis.

When anger explodes, it's too late:

- The damage has been done.
- The student has been expelled.
- The words have been said.
- The marriage is over.
- The precious keepsake is shattered.
- The police are on their way.

This book is about anger management

It offers a practical how-to approach to the experience and expression of anger.

It's about voicing anger in constructive and acceptable ways rather than bottling it up or exploding violently.

It's about developing the maturity to allow others to be angry at you, without retreating into a defensive or threatening posture yourself.

But most of all, this book is about making the healthy expression of strong emotion an expected and acceptable part of every day life.

This book is intended for family consumption

The chapters are brief and focused. The emphasis is on practical, step-by-step change, not theory.

Read on, but don't read alone. It's important that people who care about one another make these changes together as a family unit, as a work group, as a classroom or as a community.

When you begin to see that your own healthier expression of anger is accepted and returned by others, the real and permanent change can take place.

Please keep in mind

That the strategies discussed in this book may be helpful and even necessary, but may not be sufficient.

If you or someone you care about has a history of intense anger, explosive temper, destructive or violent acts, and in particular when anger is tied to substance abuse, mental illness or trauma, professional help is needed.

In each of these instances, it's critical to reach out to someone you trust:

- Your family physician
- Clergy-person
- School counselor
- Employee advocate; or
- Local mental health provider

The next explosion may be the one that does permanent damage or injury.

Don't let your fear of the next explosion stop you from making changes and seeking help now.

Anger is necessary and natural

The evolution and development of emotional control

Back in the days of the dinosaur, only the fit survived. When a drooling, smelly T. Rex approached, those among our distant ancestors who reflexively tightened their muscles, increased their heart rate, blood pressure and respiration tended to run fast enough to escape and pass those genes on to us. In the Jurassic Age, that automatic anger-fear, fight-or-flight reaction was adaptive. It kept people alive.

Today, in the Information Age, the same reflexive physical reactions are rarely necessary and more often just plain get in the way.

That reflexive heart-pounding, hyperventilating ready-to-run feeling interferes with clear thinking and mature decision-making.

Talk show hosts and glossy magazine covers have made the phrase, *"It's okay to be angry"* into a tired cliché. It may be overused, but it is true. It is okay to be angry. It is not okay to react to anger reflexively, as if every insult and criticism was the attack of a T. Rex.

It is okay to be angry.
And sad. And happy. And scared. What matters is what you do about the feeling.
From birth forward.

Human infants experience emotion as either good or bad. Happy or not-happy. Without the benefit of intellectual or physical maturity, all they can do is act on their feeling immediately.

Happy? They smile and coo and laugh. Not-happy? They scream and cry and thrash and bite.

Reflexive, unthinking behavior is called impulsive. Impulsive responses usually cause hurt and destruction, later regret and punishment.

Impulsive:

means doing without thinking. When you begin to recognize your impulsive behaviors, you can begin to control them.

**Growing up is about learning to control impulses.
To think before you act.**

It's about learning		
	1	To acknowledge that you're having a feeling
	2	To label that feeling
	3	To recognize the size of the feeling
	4	How to use this information to make healthy choices about that feeling.

In short, growing up is about learning to cope with emotions constructively.

Am I having an emotion?

This may seem like an obvious question to some, but it is a real challenge for others. Emotions are experiences inside your head that influence how you think, how you behave and how your body functions. They often (but not always) occur in response to an experience, sometimes as immediate responses and sometimes delayed by hours or days or longer.

It is often useful to figure out the Why? question: *"Why am I having this emotion?" "Why am I feeling happy (sad, mad or scared)?"*

This book, however, is not about the **Why? question.** It's about the **How? question:** How can I cope with this feeling?

What flavor is that feeling?

If someone sent you to the grocery store with instructions to purchase three pieces of fruit, you'd probably be confused.

You might reasonably ask, *"What kind?"*
The same is true of emotions.

Generic words like *upset* or *disturbed* only communicate that you're having an emotion.

That's a good start for some people. The goal is to be able to say what kind of upset.

Emotions come in four basic flavors

1	Happy
2	Sad
3	Mad
4	Scared

In fact, there are an infinite number of emotional states, but most are variations on one or more of these basic four.

Chances are you're good at determining whether you're happy or not-happy.

For most of us, the challenge is learning to identify what flavor of not-happy we're experiencing.

Chapter 6 is about trying to distinguish among the three kinds of not-happy.

TRY THIS:

You can improve your ability to identify and communicate your feeling states by giving one another pop quizzes.

Interrupt an activity and say, *"Pop quiz! What are you feeling?"* Your partner (spouse, child, parent, co-worker, friend) need only say happy, sad, mad or scared to pass the quiz.

Your job is simply to listen to the response and compliment the success expressing a feeling. Don't become defensive. Don't try to fix it. Even asking *"why?"* may be too much. **Chapter 9** is about how to respond when someone says, *"I'm mad at you!"*

Cognitive mediation

Describes the process of using words to label and better control your feelings and behaviors.

The purposeful process of looking inside yourself, labeling and measuring your own emotional state will give you enough time to recognize and side-step your impulses.

Thought requires words. Words give you a handle on your behavior. Cognitive mediation will help you make better choices.

Chapter 6 is about establishing shared labels to describe and communicate emotional states.

How big is that feeling?

Not all mad is created equal.

Once you're able to say what you're feeling, the next challenge to say how much of it you're feeling. **Chapter 5** is about learning to distinguish the experience of happy-mad-sad-scared by size.

The size of a feeling is important because as an emotion gets bigger, there is less room left for rational thought and mature decision-making.

The more mad you are, the less likely you will make healthy choices.

With this in mind, **Chapter 7** will help you make advance plans for what to do as the size of a feeling grows.

These four steps together

are the basics of emotional maturity.

1 Acknowledging

2 Labeling

3 Measuring

4 Making healthy choices

Once you and the people you care about share these skills, **any conflict can be resolved,** any trauma can be overcome in a healthy, growing way.

When anger is forbidden

Why bother with all this anger management stuff anyway?

Wouldn't it be easier to simply forbid your children from becoming angry?

You could punish them for feeling frustrated, ground them for any hint of aggravation and give time-outs for tantrums.

Why tolerate their anger at all? In any form, at any time for any reason? Children should be seen and not heard, right?

"Manage their anger?" you think, indignant. *"What do they have to be angry about? They have no right to be angry after all you do for them!"*

Wrong.

Every experience of emotion is healthy. Some expressions of emotion are not

Anger management is about learning to find socially acceptable, constructive means of expressing the necessary and natural experience of strong emotion.

Your job as a parent is to both teach your kids and model for your kids what to do with that powerful emotional energy.

> ## Forbidding anger
> only makes it go underground.

Emotional energy doesn't disappear

Much as we might like to believe that an emotion ignored will simply go away, it won't. The emotional *charge* or energy you experience has to go somewhere. Our natural response is to release it impulsively. That spontaneous, primitive expression is expectable and perhaps even acceptable for an infant, but we ask more of kids as they develop.

We ask that they fit their emotional expressions into the world we all share. It's a parent's job to shape or channel this expression.

When that channel is blocked, when it is not okay to show feelings, the feelings don't disappear, they go underground. They pool like river water accumulating behind a dam, creating one or more of three dangerous situations.

Forbidden feelings become minefields. We've all had the experience of holding feelings within, only to find ourselves super-sensitive and over-reactive to otherwise unimportant things.

When anger expression is forbidden, the emotional energy seeks any outlet available. If you can't show anger at home, you're more likely to explode at school or on the playground or with your friends.

It's the familiar story about the man frustrated at his boss but scared to let him know, so he kicks the dog at home. The emotional energy may be released, but the problem isn't solved.

Quite the contrary, the problem becomes ever more complicated by the reactions of those who accidentally step into the minefield.

Forbidden feelings become physical illnesses. Headaches and tummy-aches and dizziness and fatigue, nausea and obesity and anorexia and insomnia. Forbidden or *repressed* feelings need release.

Sometimes they find release in physical ailments. These symptoms may have an emotional cause (that is, they are *psychogenic* or *psychosomatic*) but are no less medically real than any other illness.

Ulcer and bowel problems and migraine and many gastro-intestinal diseases often are linked to or worsened by strong feelings in need of expression.

Forbidden feelings become mental illnesses. Like physical illness, many mental illnesses are believed to be due in part to genetics or biology and in part to experience and emotion.

Repressed emotions pooling within are often enough to trigger serious mental illness.

Anxiety and depression and psychosis can each result from or be worsened by strong feelings locked within.

Among children with no known family history of mental illness, unexpressed anger may be the single largest cause of depression, school failure and suicide attempts.

Intimidation and Shame

You can—and many parents in generations past have—forbidden children's anger.

It is possible to threaten and intimidate and **shame your kids into swallowing their feelings up** within themselves, smiling all the while, in order to please you or to avoid a punishment.

The antiquated *seen but not heard* philosophy of childhood discourages kids from any and all expression.

It may be that we've gone too far in the opposite direction, that we've become too permissive, too welcoming of any expression no matter how rude or destructive.

Where you draw the line on appropriate and acceptable expressions in your family is up to you, but it is important that you **draw that line clearly and enforce it consistently.**

Total, uncensored freedom can undermine a child's sense of security just as much as total repression and prohibition of expression teaches shame and may lead to serious illness.

Finding an acceptable outlet is the key

Too many parents have spent too much time telling their kids what is not okay to do when they're mad. *"Don't hit your sister!"* we yell, neglecting to suggest how best to express frustration, irritation, aggravation or rage.

This book is about recognizing anger for what it is. A natural and necessary and valuable part of the human experience, and finding healthy means of expressing it.

It's okay to be angry
This book will help you learn how to show it.

4

Is anger expression learned?
Yes and No

No,

in some ways anger expression is not learned.

Built-in, genetically determined matters of health and brain chemistry and temperament certainly play a role in how emotion is expressed in general and how anger is expressed in particular.

Some people seem to be more naturally prone to impulsive, explosive actions than others. Some seem to be more naturally withholding, internalizing or inhibited than others. But among physically and psychologically healthy people, these differences are only a small part of the story.

You should know: there are both physical and psychological conditions which play important roles in anger expression and in how effective an anger management strategy can be.

Among these are neurological difficulties including some forms of epilepsy, metabolic difficulties including hypo—and hyperthyroidism, diabetes and hypoglycemia and mental health concerns including manic-depressive (also known as bipolar) disorder and attention deficit (hyperactivity) disorder (see **Chapter 11**).

If you or someone you care about may have one or more of these **biological challenges,** it is important to consult a physician or mental health professional about how best to benefit from an anger management program.

Concurrent medication, individual or family psychotherapy will sometimes provide the additional support necessary for an anger management strategy to work.

Yes,

For most people learning plays a very important role in how emotion is acknowledged, labeled and expressed.

This means that bad habits (destructive, impulsive expressions) can be unlearned. It also means that your choices may be influencing how the people you care about learn to express their own emotions.

You are a model to your kids

One of the most important factors in learning how to express emotion is your example as a parent. Expect that your kids will do as you do, not as you say.

This means that you must practice what you preach.

Do you know when you're experiencing an emotion?

Do you have words to label these emotions? Do you recognize your emotions when they're still small, or do you seem to go from zero to 60 in an instant? What do you do when you get mad? Happy? Scared? Sad? Expect the same from your kids.

Double standards don't work.

It's not enough to say, *"I can because I'm the parent."* Whether or not they admit it, your kids want to be just like you. **Think about it:** How often have you looked in the mirror and seen your mom or dad?

Don't pretend they don't see and hear you.

Kids have amazing antennae. Assume that you are constantly being observed, no matter how involved they seem to be in their play, no matter how loud they seem to be snoring, no matter how quiet you think you are and how distant they seem to be.

They know. They're tuned in to your emotions long before they understand your words, and they will do as you do, every time.

What works?

Behaviors that are rewarded, are repeated

If a particular emotion expression is functional, if it achieves a desirable outcome or consequence, it will be repeated.

This means that you must not allow yourself to be emotionally blackmailed.

Too often, tired and frustrated parents set limits, *"No, you cannot stay up until 10 p.m.!"* and then back down in the face of an onslaught of whining or tantruming or worse.

Every time you give in, you are teaching your children to behave in the same way ten or a hundred or a thousand more times.

BOTTOM LINE

If you set a limit, stick to it. If there's room for negotiation, there can be no discussion until everyone involved is acting in a calm and mature and reasonable manner.

Squeaky wheels

A related part of the *"What works...?"* formula for learning how to express emotions is the squeaky-wheel-gets-the-oil phenomenon.

1 Everyone is busy.
It's easy to ignore your kids and others you care about when everything is running smoothly.

Imagine, however, that your attention is the precious fuel that keeps the family going

2 If you pay little attention to good behavior but you stop and pay attention (scold, scream, punish) to unacceptable behavior (fighting, failing in school, in trouble with the law), then you are oiling the wheel that squeaks.

You are actually rewarding misbehavior.

3 Put down the device.
Turn off the cell phone and the computer and the TV.

Make time to listen to your kids now, while they're succeeding. Oil the wheel that DOES NOT squeak.

4 If you show an interest in their achievement, friends and goals, you will oil the wheel while it works well, and it may never squeak.

TRY THIS...

The best model for limit setting comes from the highway patrol. Every highway is posted with speed limits. Every car has a speedometer.

If you choose to go faster than the limit, you are taking a risk. If you are stopped, the officer is (supposed to be) calm and cool and collected.

The officer asks if you were aware that you were speeding, collects your identification, writes out a ticket according to established (and sometimes posted) standards, and calmly sends you on your way.

Your whining and pleading and begging and crying does nothing (except perhaps worsen this situation).

You can do the same.
If you bring emotion to limit setting you will fuel your child's emotional reaction. If you are calm and consistent, you will help your child be calm and mature and you will teach your kids that you cannot be emotionally blackmailed.

Your emotions matter, too

Finally, expect that your emotional reactions to your kids' emotions communicate a lot.

Do you genuinely believe that it's okay to be mad? Is it okay for your kids to be mad at you? (See Chapters 3 and 9.)

Do you turn away in disgust or embarrassment or frustration when your son or daughter expresses a feeling? Does your discomfort come across as ridicule? Condemnation? Uncaring? Do you believe that boys shouldn't cry?

These responses tell kids to bury their feelings underground (see Chapter 3). They suggest that it's not okay to express their anger/sadness/fear directly.

Instead, the emotional energy gets redirected and will appear some place else, less directly, less constructively and in a less mature form.

If you understand that your kids are struggling to learn to master their own emotions, then you understand that your emotions can overwhelm and disorient them.

Being able to remain calm and reasonable in the face of a child's strong emotions can be as difficult as it is important.

In order to teach your kids to express strong emotions including anger in the most mature, healthy and constructive form, you have to be prepared to be the target of these feelings.

If you take these expressions personally, if your kids fear that their feelings can make you go away, stop loving them, get drunk, argue with their other parent(s), then they will not feel safe bringing their feelings to you.

TRY THIS...

Listen for the feelings in every communication first, before you listen for the content of the message.

This will feel awkward at first. It may make you uncomfortable or embarrassed, but it is the single best way to build healthy relationships and encourage healthy emotion expression.

When you can respond to any statement by labeling the expressed feeling:
"I hear that you're mad"
you'll defuse the worst of conflicts and often avoid a lot of unnecessary talk about unimportant things.

What to do
Anger by degrees:
The MadMeter™

If you're like most people, you often resist voicing your feelings until it's too late. You sit by politely, embarrassed or uncertain or nervous or simply unaware that you're having a feeling, tolerating as much as you can tolerate alone and in silence until you cross a critical threshold and explode like an over-inflated balloon.

This can be true of any emotional experience, but it is probably most true about anger.

Emotion is energy

One of two things happens to your unexpressed emotional energy.

For some, bottled up feelings are turned inward, becoming self-destructive. Anger unexpressed toward others is expressed toward oneself. It becomes headaches and stomachaches, ulcers and bowel problems. It damages self-esteem and can motivate self-destructive acts and suicide attempts. Turning anger inward is one certain recipe for depression.

For others, the bottled up or repressed feelings accumulate like air in a quickly expanding balloon. One breath at a time the balloon gets bigger until all it takes is one last little pin-prick of emotion for the whole package to explode.

The anger expression that erupts at that point is dramatically out of proportion to the incident that set it off. This kind of explosion is often destructive or violent or abusive. It often pushes people away, leads to regret and loss and punishment.

The key to avoiding both of these outcomes is learning to recognize and adequately voice the strong emotion—especially the anger—anger that naturally occurs every day.

As with anything else, this skill requires daily practice (see Chapter 10). Learning to acknowledge and express your strong feelings will require that you develop new ways of thinking and talking (see Chapter 6) and invent an entirely new metric for measuring your experience of emotion.

Emotion by the numbers

The MadMeter™ is a tool intended to help you begin to think about emotions by degrees. It is a simple **1 to 10 scale,** where ten represents the greatest extreme of an emotional state possible.

FOR SADNESS
10 is desperate, crippling grief.

FOR FEAR
10 is mind-numbing, pants-wetting, bone-chilling terror.

FOR HAPPINESS
10 is euphoric, grandiose, jubilant joy.

FOR ANGER
10 is volcanic, nuclear, seeing-red, insane, all-consuming rage.

Hands very close together, palm-to-palm, represents **1** on the MadMeter™, the least recognizable degree of a feeling.

Spread your hands further and further apart to span **2, 3, 4, 5, 6 ...**

BY ANALOGY
Consider the tachometer on your car. The engine races through each gear, increasing RPM until you shift (or the engine shifts for you) into a higher gear. When speed outstrips a gear, the engine revs faster and faster into a red-line zone, the range in which damage will occur. As with emotions, **the goal is to remain below that critical range.** For younger children and those with learning difficulties, numbers can be difficult.

One is the least little drip of a feeling, the seed from which the full flower of grief or terror or joy or rage might grow.

The numbers in between represent successive degrees of emotion, where seven is the threshold beyond which thinking stops and emotion takes over.

No matter the person or the feeling state (happy, sad, mad or scared), any emotion approaching **eight, nine and ten** predictably hurt themselves and others, destroy property and later come to regret their actions.

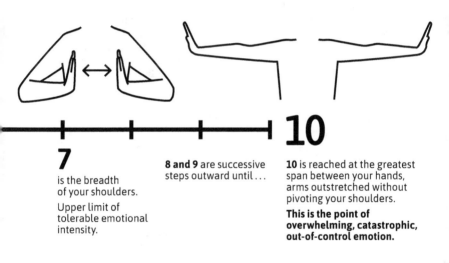

7

is the breadth of your shoulders.

Upper limit of tolerable emotional intensity.

8 and 9 are successive steps outward until . . .

10 is reached at the greatest span between your hands, arms outstretched without pivoting your shoulders.

This is the point of overwhelming, catastrophic, out-of-control emotion.

Acknowledging the crumbs of emotion

One of the keys to avoiding those undesirable 8-, 9- and 10-Mad states is learning to talk about the 1's and 2's and 3's.

But society so often tells us to ignore these things. *"Don't sweat the small stuff"* they all say.

True, the purpose is not to make mountains out of molehills, not to dwell on things better passed over.

It may be enough to recognize the presence of an irritant, the kindling that could later start a bonfire, the first breaths of air that begin to inflate that fragile balloon of temper.

How? With words

Purposefully, consciously putting a feeling into words is like putting a leash on an unfamiliar dog. The animal might be well-trained and obedient, but just in case he tries to run off or gets out-of-control, you have a way to stop him.

If you're able to say *"I'm 3-Mad"* inside your head or out loud to yourself, you'll be better prepared when the next irritant comes along.

You'll be more likely to control your behavior and make healthy, safe choices.

Applying words to your emotional experience will help you begin to contain impulses, control behavior and will help you model the better choices for your children.

"I'm 5-Mad"

"I'm 3-Mad"

Establishing a plan

The MadMeter™ creates the opportunity to establish predictable action plans corresponding to the size of an emotional state. With a little planning ahead, the ability to say, *"I'm 3-Mad"* or *"I'm 6-Mad"* or even, *"I'm 9-Mad,"* can open the door for specific responses.

HERE ARE SOME EXAMPLES:

7–10 Mad ↓	**Danger! Immediate action is necessary to avoid an explosion!** Use a safe outlet to vent the anger energy (see Chapter 7). Ask for help if you need it: *"I can't be alone right now. I need help."* **Don't make decisions.** Don't drive a car, ride a bike or do anything that could endanger yourself or others. You're not thinking clearly.
4–6 Mad ↓	**Take time to *chill out*** Get your feelings back to a manageable size (see Chapter 7). Consider writing or drawing.
1–3 Mad	**Say how you feel: *"I'm 2-Mad!"*** Expect others to listen (see Chapter 9). Can you say why you are mad? *"I'm 3-Mad because you won't give me that toy!"*

The MadMeter™ is also useful for debriefing after an anger incident (see Chapter 8). Later, after the dust has settled and the upset is past, it's useful to talk about actions and reactions in terms of degree of anger.

Learning that particular words or behavior incites a certain degree of anger can help avoid future confrontations.

For example: *"You made me 6-Mad when you called me that name"* opens up responses like, *"I was 8-Mad when I swore at you."* You can ask, *"What should you have done instead if you were that mad?"* and *"Did you see when you were 5-Mad and 6-Mad? How could you have avoided letting it get even bigger?"*

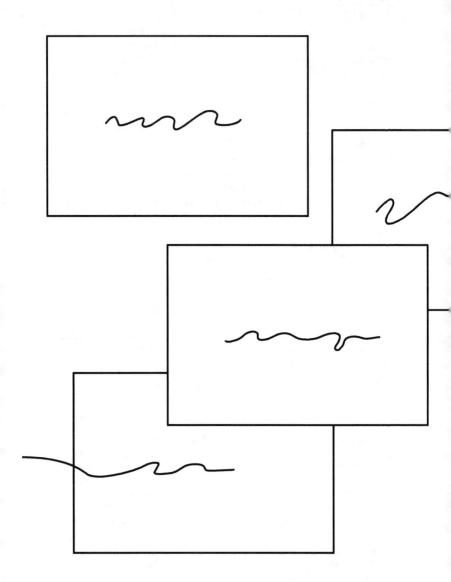

What to do
Establish an anger vocabulary

Languages change over time. In the same way that living things evolve to adapt to their environments, words evolve to serve the needs of speakers.

Native American Eskimos, for example, have developed an entire vocabulary to describe snow conditions. Soft-and-fluffy. Icy-glazed. Hard-packed.

Because these distinctions can determine when and where you travel, what you wear and what you can do, they have developed clear ways to communicate important differences.

Unfortunately, our language fails to do the same with emotions. Even though the differences between feeling states can be just as important in determining behavior as weather conditions, our shared vocabulary for emotions is woefully inadequate.

You can prove this by asking any three people to rank order the relative degree of anger expressed by these three words:

Frustrated, Aggravated and *Irritated.* No two will agree.

In fact, there are no right answers to questions like this. Some people hear *"frustrated"* and think 8-Mad (on a 10 point scale, see Chapter 5). Others take the same word to suggest 2-Mad.

So long as you and the people you care about use words like these differently, behavior will be unpredictable, communication will be poor and conflicts will erupt unnecessarily.

Agree on a vocabulary. Because there is no absolute right and wrong about the meaning of most feeling words, and because this ambiguity causes unnecessary confusion and conflict, you must create your own definitions.

Once you and the people you care about have created your own shared vocabulary for emotions, you can begin to better predict and control the behaviors accompanying the feelings.

The Anger Line

1   **Call** everyone together for a family meeting.
Pass out note cards and pencils.

---

2   **Brainstorm** every word that you can think of that is associated
with anger. Write each one down on a note card.

---

3   **Review** the entire collection of anger words.

Veto the words that you find unacceptable, obscene or
provocative. Be careful to avoid generic words like *upset* which
suggest the generic *not-happy* to most people.

Here's a brief list to get you started:

*Mad - Enraged - Irritated - Frustrated - Aggravated - Annoyed - Incensed
- Angry - Bothered - Furious*

---

4   **Sort** the note cards into an order that makes sense to you as a
group, from least powerful anger to most powerful anger.

You can do this most effectively by asking about pairs of words,
for example: "Which do we think is more angry, *frustrated*
or *irritated*?" There are no right or wrong answers and not
everyone will agree.

Make decisions based on majority consensus.

---

5   **Create** a horizontal number line, from 1 through 10. Leave
space beneath each number for a word. **If you're artistic**, make
the numbers appear larger and more colorful as they approach
10 to suggest the idea that the associated feelings are getting
larger and more powerful as the numbers become larger.

---

6   **Assign** the labels on the cards to the numbers in the order in
which you've sorted them so that the least powerful word is
assigned to 1, and so on, up to 10. If you have more than 10
words, it's okay to discard those that seem unnecessary, or to
have more than one word for some numbers.

---

7   **Post** the Anger Line some place visible in your home,
classroom or workplace. **Refer to it** often as you gradually fine
tune your anger expression vocabulary.

What to do

What is okay to do when you're mad?

You now have three essential tools for dealing with anger:

1 You're able to acknowledge that you're experiencing an emotion

2 You're able to measure how big that emotion is

3 You're able to label and communicate your emotional state

Most people have spent a lot of time and energy figuring out what's not okay to do when you're angry

Parents tend to lecture and yell about not yelling, not hitting your sister, not swearing and such.

Teachers and principals tend to respond to unacceptable angry behavior by handing out detentions and suspensions and expulsions.

Society in general tends to simply punish what is unacceptable with courts and fines, jails and prisons, with little or no attention paid to what is okay to do when you're mad.

The question remains:

What is okay to do with your anger?

Plan ahead

Anger happens. Pretending that nothing will ever irritate, frustrate or aggravate you is simple denial. Better to plan ahead now in anticipation of the anger that will inevitably occur (see Chapters 2 and 10), than to wait until the crisis erupts and find that you have no plans in place.

Within the limits of safety, the anger expressions that you decide to endorse are entirely up to you. The examples spelled out in this book are only examples. You and the people you care about must determine what works for you.

Age and maturity will be part of the formula. Younger and less mature people will value more physical and immediate outlets, while older and more mature individuals should be encouraged to be less impulsive and to use more symbolic and expressive outlets (talking or writing, for example).

Your beliefs will also play a role in determining which anger outlets are acceptable. Hitting a pillow, for example, may seem like an acceptable alternative to violence in some homes while others see it as too aggressive. Screaming may be a successful step away from swearing or kicking in some settings but be seen as totally unacceptable in others.

Catharsis?

That's the word that suggests that a person can vent feelings about somebody else harmlessly by doing something like hitting a pillow or playing a shoot-em-up video game.

It's a popular view and it may work for you, but the evidence suggests that it's wrong.

Scientific studies demonstrate that adult endorsements and modeling of activities like hitting a punching bag and killing space invaders actually increases children's aggressive behaviors.

This means that, whenever possible, it's best to recommend non-destructive, non-aggressive means of expressing anger.

Chill-out

The first step in planning ahead for anger is to give permission to step away from conflict. Different than the much misunderstood *time out*, chill out can be your code word meant to express that, *"I'm 5-Mad and getting madder quickly. If this keeps going I'm going to explode. I'm going to take a 5-minute break to calm down and then we can try this again."*

Being able to chill out requires mutual agreement to the terms of the idea well in advance, it requires the maturity to look inside and recognize an explosive situation before it happens and it requires the skill to calm down once you're away from the conflict.

The 5-minute break idea is a critical part of chill out. It's not enough to simply walk away from a conflict (although that may be better than some other choices).

Chill-out requires a firm commitment to return shortly. Particularly because anger and conflict routinely make all involved feel more needy and less secure, it's important to communicate that, *"I'm not abandoning you. I'm taking a break. I'll be back in 5 minutes."*

It may even be important to say where you'll be while you're chilling out: *"I'm going to have a cold glass of water in the kitchen. I'll meet you back here in 5 minutes."*

Yes, some younger children will follow you, unable to disengage. They'll need a number of repetitions to understand what you're doing when you take a chill out.

Try not to get angry at them for following you. If necessary, restate your intention calmly.
"I came in here to calm down because I was getting too mad. It's eight-zero-zero on the clock here. At eight-zero-five I'll meet you back in the family room so we can try to talk some more."

No, you can not get the last word in. Unless there is an immediate threat to safety, the conflict must come to a screeching halt as soon as a chill out is requested. It's hard, but it's necessary.

And yes, you do have to **be careful that chill out isn't misused** to manipulate or procrastinate. The first time that you suspect that a child is requesting a chill out for the wrong reasons, let it go until later, when the conflict is past.

Try to talk about it calmly, redefine the idea of chill out and give her or him another chance. If the manipulative behavior persists, you may not be ready for chill out.

The mad box

When kids can't talk about a subject as provocative as their own anger face-to-face, it's possible to have the conversation in other ways.

Creating a Mad Box can be useful in at least two ways. First, the actual shared process of creating the Mad Box can open up the topic of anger expression.

Talking about anger in the context of a shared activity is often less threatening than sitting down face-to-face.

By working together to create a Mad Box the family is making a very clear statement that anger is okay. Second, the Mad Box itself, once in place, offers a predictable, acceptable place to take anger when it occurs.

HERE'S WHAT TO DO:

1 Find a medium sized cardboard box with a lid. The typical 9x11x17 inch box in which reams of paper are delivered is a great size and is free from many copy stores.

2 Decorate the box together in the medium of your choice. Crayons, ink, paint, glue. Label it, **Mad Box** and invite anger-related artwork.

3 Brainstorm and list all the outlets for anger that are acceptable in your family and can be stored in the box. Include some vents for physical energy (Play-doh to pound, a sponge-ball for squeezing, old newspapers for balling up, shredding and scribbling on) and some vents for more sophisticated and mature (crayons for coloring, a notepad and pen for writing).

Other choices include an empty milk jug that can be screamed into, balloons for blowing, batting, bopping or exploding and tissues for crying.

4 Decide where the **Mad Box** belongs. Pick a highly visible, commonly used place. The TV room? The hall between the bedrooms? The back of the van?

5 Use it yourself. Be a model of healthy anger expression. Use the **Mad Box** when your anger starts to build. If you think it's silly and don't use it, neither will your kids.

Rewards and punishments

The punishments are plentiful.
Most kids know how to push your buttons when they're angry, and some discover that pushing your buttons is the only way to get your precious time and attention.

(see Chapter 4 about "Squeaky Wheels").

Genuine rewards for positive and mature anger expressions are harder to implement but are very much preferable. Rewarding successes tends to build self-esteem, create incentive for future successes and enhance the cooperative, positive environment at home, in the classroom or in the workplace.

Reward programs intended to modify children's expressions of anger can be used with any age group in any setting.

It is critical, however, that the program to be used is carefully planned, consistently implemented and meaningful to the child. *The meaningful to the child* requirement stumps a lot of caregivers who hear "*I don't care*" over and over again. Often, "*I don't care*" is meaningless.

What matters is whether the rewards built into your program are valuable to the child.

Token economy

Here's one way to implement an Anger Management Reward Program called a token economy.

Identify goal behaviors:
What behaviors are you trying to change? How will you recognize success?

Start with the behaviors you face every day and set goals just a notch or two higher. It may not be reasonable to ask a child who is hitting, kicking and biting to talk about his anger at first. That child may need to start with *no violent contact*, even if that means that swearing or sticking out his tongue is rewarded as a success until violence is absent and the goals can be shifted.

A child who is swearing might be rewarded for no swearing, even if he is still yelling, and so on.

Identify reward places and periods:
When and where will this program be in force? Just in your home? Only while in your company? At Dad's house, too? At school? Can you start by changing behavior only during one part of the day?

Between supper and bedtime?
Between wake-up and school?

In general, the more narrowly you define the times and places you are monitoring, the more likely the child will succeed.

Start small. Target no more than 2-3 specific behaviors. Monitor these for no more than 2-3 hours in one setting only. Once you have some success, you can begin to slowly expand goals or times or settings.

Identify tokens.
Tokens must be unique, non-counterfeitable, specific to each child and pocket-size. Poker chips generally work well.

If you are trying to shape behavior of more than one child at the same time, assign one color chip to each child to minimize the, *"that's my chip!"* complaints.

Identify rewards.
Brainstorm everything the child(ren) ever wanted, from a piece of bubble gum to a trip to Disney World.

Help them identify some things that are relatively large, medium and small. Use your parental veto to eliminate unacceptable items (weapons, for example).

Assign token values to each remaining item. By creating a prize menu, you can help your kids learn to delay gratification by saving up success tokens and you can gratify the most impulsive *"I want it now!"* child with a daily trinket.

Beware of reward inflation!
Set your token values carefully. If your son is eligible to earn a maximum of 5 tokens a day, the smallest (least expensive, least effort-demanding) prize might be worth 5 tokens.

If you believe that this same child should earn a fast food lunch no more than once a week, set that prize equal to **30 tokens** (7 days times maximum 5 tokens per day equals 35; 30 allows some error over the course of the week).

Huge prizes like a $70 500-piece Lego set can be earned one piece at a time.

Consistency and follow-through.
If there are other caregivers involved during the times you are rewarding or in the places you are rewarding, they must be informed. You and these co-parents must follow through every single time.

Do not take away tokens that have been earned for later misbehavior. The success is still a success. You can, however, decide whether to open the prize *store* for *shopping* depending on a child's successes that day.

Punish as a last resort.
A program like this does not replace punishment. It aims to create a more desirable choice than those behaviors which earn punishments.

A child who fails to earn a potential reward might still require punishment.

What to do

Acknowledging the deed: Debriefing

If words are part of the key to learning to control and appropriately express anger, then you must start talking about angry incidents.

No more ignoring last night's explosion, pretending it didn't happen. **No more** minimizing—making a mountain into a molehill to avoid confrontation or embarrassment or to protect someone.

Talking about an angry incident after the fact is not a punishment. It's not about shame or even remorse. It's about learning to maker better choices in the future.

The ability to admit your own mistakes and poor choices requires a certain degree of maturity.

Most preschoolers and immature grade-schoolers avoid and deny responsibility for their own actions, preferring to scapegoat and blame others. *"I didn't do it!"* is a favorite claim, *"It was all his fault!"*

The truth is that few, if any, conflicts are entirely the fault of only one participant.

Learning to recognize your own misbehavior and developing the maturity to admit to these mistakes is part of becoming better able to avoid future mistakes.

If you can help your kids recognize and talk about their own mistakes, they will have the words to begin to make changes.

Own Your Actions

That's The First Rule.

Emotion corrupts thinking

Remember that the stronger your emotion, the less clearly you are thinking.

Two people with strong emotion have a cumulative effect.
If you're 5-Mad and your son is 5-Mad, the combined emotional energy is at least 10-Mad, a state that is likely out-of- control and possibly dangerous.

Chill-out.
Use your Mad Box.
Use your words.
Come back to talking after the emotional energy is calmed.

Acknowledge your own choices without blaming others.

"I kicked her" is a much more mature and constructive statement than *"I kicked her because she kicked me first!"*

Beware of your own emotions

Your anger, fear, embarrassment and frustration show. Your feelings leak out as emotional energy which effects your kids, even though you think your emotions are well controlled.

Together with their own overpowering emotions, this energy adds to the confusion.

Take a chill out. So long as everyone is safe, most situations can wait until your emotions are better under control.

Talking it through requires ownership.

"It's not fair!" and "I hate you"

Are two of the most common and provocative lines among children everywhere. **If you respond to either at face value,** the battle is lost.

"It's not fair"	The answer is, *"Yes. You're right. It's not fair. Can you tell me how you feel?"* Explaining, *"When I was your age I had to..."* Misses the point.	The point is about feelings. Anger? Resentment? Jealousy? **Talk about the feelings and you may change the future.**
"I hate you"	Works the same way. Taken at face value, it pushes a lot of adult buttons. In truth, most children really mean, *"I'm 10-Mad at you!"*	When they realize that these words get you going, they're likely to say them more and more. **Respond by reframing the idea,** *"I understand that you're 10-Mad at me..."* and next time you may hear *"I don't know"*.
"I don't know"	Is another favorite that rarely means what you expect. If you take *"I don't know"* as a lie because you know that he does know, you're likely to add to your own frustration.	**Start with a critical distinction** that most kids need coaching to see: *"Do you mean you don't know or do you mean that you don't want to talk about it?"* A child who can clarify that he, in fact, meant that he knows but doesn't want to talk about it has given you an opening. **You might try:** *"Okay. Can you at least tell me why you don't want to talk about it?"*

Confessions of embarrassment, regret, remorse and even continued anger are often all that is necessary to open the discussion.

Whenever possible, go slow. Take the child's lead in words, in emotions and even in posture. You'll get further talking about anything emotional sitting side-by-side than face on, minimizing the pressure of confrontation.

The "After Words"

Is a simple format for debriefing after an anger outburst. It is a predictable, consistent structure which can help kids begin to use words to explain and later to control their own actions.

"AFTER WORDS" ASKS FOUR SIMPLE QUESTIONS:

1   What was the argument or fight about?

2   What did I do wrong?

3   What did I do right?

4   What will I do differently next time?

Children from age 5 years on can learn to expect to answer these four questions after an explosion. **By 7 or 8** most can write their answers out on paper or talk them through face-to-face or into a tape recorder.

TRY THIS IF AN ARGUMENT OR FIGHT ERUPTS

1. **Separate the participants.** Use your own familiar time out or go-to-your-room strategy.

2. **Put privileges and events on hold** until each child is able to answer the "After Words" questions to your satisfaction.

3. Take care to **create reasonable expectations** for each child by age and ability.

4. **Collect the "After Words"** pages in a binder so that you can look back later.

YOU MIGHT PROMPT

"Remember last time this happened? What did you say you'd do differently next time? Did you do that this time? Why not? Let's try again next time."

What to do
How do you respond to others' anger?

Anger is often the scariest, most destructive and confusing of all of our emotions.
Learning how to accept and express anger takes many of us a lifetime. How then, are we supposed to respond when our kids have the guts to say, *"I'm mad at you!"*

A. Get mad back at him

Wrong. If a statement like, *"I'm mad at you."* provokes your anger, at least two things are true. First, your fuse is too short. If you have any hope of teaching your kids good anger management strategies, it's time to learn some yourself. Find a self-help book, counselor, minister or good friend to help you manage your anger so that he can learn to manage his.

Second, your anger will only fuel his anger and vice-versa in an upward spiral of increasing rage. The potential for reasonable, healthy interaction decreases and the likelihood of destructive and

violent acts increases when anger spirals out-of-control.

If you find yourself getting mad at your child for being mad at you, take a step back. Model self-control. Try saying, *"I don't think we can talk about this right now. Let's try again [when? Be specific!] after we've both cooled down."*

B. "If you think you're mad now, I'll give you something to be mad about!"

Wrong again. Your child is entitled to her or his anger, no matter what its source. This vaguely masked threat may succeed in intimidating your child out of expressing her or his anger at that moment, but it does nothing for the anger itself. Instead, this response suggests that only the big and strong are allowed to express their anger while everyone else is forced to let their anger fester within.

What's wrong with that?
Emotions need to be vented. It takes energy to hold strong feelings inside, energy that is better spent learning and growing and exploring.

Anger held within causes many people to become depressed, to develop physical complaints and creates the risk that the pent up feelings will later explode in some disproportionate, destructive way.

C. *"I'm sorry to hear that."*

This is more empathic, but just as wrong. It sounds like the sort of empty condolence you might give a passing acquaintance over her grandmother's death.

This response simultaneously dismisses the child's anger as trivial and criticizes him for expressing it.

The only place for apology is if you believe that you genuinely did something wrong that angered your child. If this is your goal, say it directly: *"I'm sorry that I broke your toy"* but say it later, after you've found the single best way to respond to your son's anger.

D. *"Why are you mad at me?"*

This is also a useful thing to ask later, but as a first response, it misses the emotional connection entirely.

It's reasonable for you to want to know what you may have done to anger your child, it may even be reasonable to try to avoid doing so in the future, but your logical analysis has to take a back seat to your empathy and compassion.

E. *"Don't talk back to me, young man!"*

This and a dozen other punitive responses may have their place in responding to those disrespectful utterances we parents call *attitude, being rude* and *talking back*, but they have no place here.

No matter where you draw the line on respect for one's elders, an honest *"I'm mad at you"* has to be acceptable. True, said with sarcasm or venom, screamed above the slam of the door or uttered as a veiled threat, you have every reason to punish, but pulling rank in the face of a child's sincere effort to express a strong feeling will surely discourage his future efforts at mature expressions of emotion.

F. *"It's okay to be mad."*

Very empathic. Very open. Very generic.

This response sounds like something you read in a popular psychology book and your kids will sense that. *"It's okay to be mad"* is a true statement and an important idea, but usually one best left unsaid in the heat of the moment or introduced later, after the storm has passed.

Right there with an angry child looking you in the face, better to be genuine and supportive than play amateur shrink.

G. *"I hear that you're angry."*

Less generic. Very empathic.

This response succeeds in avoiding the defensive power struggles implicit in many natural responses to *"I'm angry at you."* It gives permission for the child to express feelings in healthy and appropriate ways, but it's still not the best first reply.

Use this line when all else fails. It expresses understanding without criticism or condescension and gives permission to say more.

But best of all:

H. *"Thank you for telling me."*

Succinct. To the point. Validates without becoming generic but most important, this response rewards the child's efforts. If you can see *"I'm mad at you"* as a developmental success, a success of impulse control and maturity, a success in not swearing at you, not spitting at you, not hitting or kicking or biting you, then it is an effort worth rewarding and your thanks are the reward.

If you understand that the behaviors that you reward are most likely to be repeated, then you recognize *"Thanks for telling me"* as the single best first response to the child who is mature enough to approach you and say, *"I'm mad at you!"*

And after that?

If the anger energy is high, it needs an outlet before many more constructive words can be expected.

What's okay to do when you're angry in your home? Punch a pillow? Shred old newspapers? Exercise? Shoot hoops? Scribble with crayons? Pound Play-doh?

Any non-violent physical activity that suits your family values and depletes the anger energy will work.

Don't wait for the crisis to look for an outlet, talk it through in advance. Sit down with the family at a calm moment and ask, *"What is okay to do when we get angry at each other?"*

Later, when the anger is manageable, when the child seems more rational and better able to talk, try, *"Can we talk about it?"* You may find that eye contact intimidates kids in this situation.

Try instead to stare at your shoes, fidget aimlessly with a toy or sit side by side facing the same blank wall, then talk.

Go at his pace
Use your empathy and maturity. Don't become defensive. **Remember what a success it is that he's talking at all.**

$\longrightarrow$

And if you don't get it right next time?

Don't worry. Accepting that your child can be angry at you is a tough step for any parent.

So long as you're not punitive, so long as you don't shame her or his feelings underground, you'll always get another chance to get it right.

When you do, when you can stop in the face of your child's healthy expression of anger and say, *"Thanks for telling me"* first, you'll find that working through anger can be a healthy, growing family experience.

Every communication has at least two parts:

The content and the associated feeling.

Too often, responding to the content alone misses the boat. The real message is in the unspoken but implied emotion.

The challenge is to listen for the feeling and to know when and how to respond to it.

"Pass the salt," for example, can be a completely benign request for a condiment at the dinner table. Usually, finding and passing the salt shaker is exactly the right response.

Sometimes, however, **"PASS THE SALT!"** is a means of expressing anger, or—said in a trembling, weak voice—can be an expression of sadness or fear.

Do pass the salt anyway, but take the time to be aware of the emotion. "I guess you're pretty mad, huh?" might help get to the root of the matter.

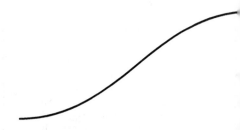

What to do
Start managing anger today

There's going to be anger. Are you prepared?

People think least clearly and act least maturely in the heat of strong emotion. It's not okay to wait until the crisis hits, to wait until you're screaming and the kids are screaming and violence could erupt at any moment. At times like those, everyone overreacts. You do and say things that you'll later regret. Decisions made in the heat of anger routinely lead to more anger, destruction and violence.

Prepare now

Read through these chapters now, while you're calm.

Pick and choose the *"What to Do?"* chapters (5-10) that make sense for you and your family, then call a family meeting to create a **Family Anger Management Plan.**

Invite everyone's input. Consider every suggestion seriously. Write out the final plan clearly and post it or give copies to everyone.

Every plan
should have at least these parts:

1. **Reassurance** that it's okay to feel angry (as well as sad, happy and scared).
2. **Clarification** about what IS okay to say (Chapter 6) and do (Chapter 7) when you're mad.
3. **Clarification** about consequences: Will a family member be punished for expressing anger in an acceptable way?
4. How will a family member be punished for expressing anger in an unacceptable way?
5. **If a conflict escalates,** how can a family member step out of it to calm down? (See "Chill Out," Chapter 7).
6. **How will the family learn from conflicts?** (See Chapter 8).

Sample Anger Management Plan

1. It's okay to be angry.
2. Some ways of showing anger are acceptable. Others are not.
3. Vent the energy safely.
4. Use your words, not your body.
5. Always be respectful, even in anger.
6. Talk, then listen.
7. If you can't talk or listen, take a 5-minute chill out, then go back to #4.
8. Afterwards, talk through the After Words questions.

Firefighters have the right idea. Local fire departments commonly visit elementary school classrooms to teach fire prevention. Extinguishers and matches, flames and electric. Make a plan in advance, they counsel, just in case there's a fire.

Practice every day

It's like swimming, regular practice builds muscles and skills. If you had to jump in, you'd be prepared. If you wait for a flood, you'll drown. Feelings work the same way. By making the expression of strong feelings a part of the daily routine, you'll build the muscles and skills necessary to cope with anger effectively when the emotions begin to flood in.

Here's how:

---

1. Listen for feelings

They're everywhere, all around you, but learning to hear and acknowledge the feelings implicit in every day communication takes time and effort.

Keep in mind that every statement has two parts:

The content and the emotion. The next time someone you care about says something to you, no matter how trivial, stop before you respond to the content and ask what was the emotion?

At least half of your kids' statements to you are really requests for help with their feelings. The classic, *"It's not fair,"* for example, invites you into a bottomless pit if you respond to the content (*"When I was little, I..."* and *"Last Thursday, he..."* and *"When you're older, you'll..."*).

You can avoid all of this and cut to the real matter at hand by saying, *"I can see that you're really mad (sad/jealous/scared/resentful)."*

2. Make it part of the routine.

Find a time each day (or, less ideally, each week) when the family is together. Supper or breakfast. Bedtime. Sunday brunch.

Ask everyone present to name something that happened that day/week that made them feel happy, sad, mad and scared.

Part of the challenge is recognizing those times that we feel each of these strong feelings to lesser degrees.

Most people are rarely enraged (10 on a 1-10 anger scale), for example, but are often irritated, frustrated or aggravated (in the 1-4 range on the same scale).

Another challenge is to encourage these expressions without challenging or jumping in to fix a feeling.

When Billy offers, *"I was really mad at you,"* how do you best respond? Offer your *"Thank you for telling me"* (see Chapter 9) without becoming defensive or punitive and encourage him to say more.

3. Use feelings to debrief and plan ahead.

Yet another way to make feeling expression a part of daily life is to focus on feelings rather than behavior and events to debrief together.

Debriefing is what you do spontaneously after spending time apart:

"What did you do at school today?" *"How was the party?"* and *"What happened at dad's this weekend?"*

You can minimize the number of *"I don't know"* and *"nothing"* answers, get more valuable information and be less intrusive by asking about feelings.

"Anything happen at school that made you happy? Proud? Frustrated?"

Do the same to orient the family to upcoming events:.

"What can you do if you start to feel frustrated at this meeting?" *"Let's make a plan just in case you start to feel sad while I'm gone...."*

11

When anger is genuinely out-of-control

Anger can be scary. Angry people can be intimidating or threatening, loud or obnoxious, destructive or violent or self-abusive. Anger impairs judgment, impedes maturity and compromises rational thought. It causes some people to cower in fear and provokes others to fight.

As real and threatening as anger can be, it is rarely *out-of-control*.

By definition, physically and psychologically healthy people age three and older who are not under the influence of alcohol, medication or illicit *street* drugs and who have not experienced severe trauma or stress are generally able to control their emotional expression.

This means that anger management strategies like those presented here can be useful to help healthy children and adults become better able to rein in destructive and violent impulses, to learn to step back from 8-, 9- and 10-Mad states to *chill out* (see Chapter 7) and to use words to talk through anger constructively.

What is *out-of-control*?

It is the inability to contain the impulse to act in a violent or destructive manner. It is the tendency to lash out with words or actions without consideration of consequences. Psychologically, it is a failure of the capacity to soothe oneself, to delay gratification and make mature choices about anger expression.

Have you ever been out-of-control?

Probably not.

The test is this: At the height of your rage (9- or 10-Mad on a 1-10 scale, see Chapter 5), could you have calmed in order to earn one million dollars? Most people say "yes" about most instances.

Those who do not, those whose anger is routinely so overwhelming that they cannot calm in order to earn something of tremendous value, can be said to be genuinely out-of-control.

These people seem unable to contain their emotions. They lash out impulsively, can't tolerate a simple "no," are prone to acts of destruction and violence.

As children, these are the kids whose violence leads to suspension or expulsion from preschools, an experience which may ensure the safety of those others enrolled but which often damages the offending child's self-esteem, increase stress for that child's family and can contribute to a cycle of escalating violence.

As children in grade school and high school, out-of-control anger often leads to school failure, depression and anti-social acts.

These kids tend to be familiar to school and community authorities and easily fall into the trap of living up to their negative reputations, a downward spiral which can lead to substance abuse and criminal charges.

Who is *out-of-control*?

Individuals whose anger routinely becomes out-of-control generally fall into one or more of four categories: As a result of substance reaction, misuse or abuse, due to immaturity, due to psychological illness and due to physical injury or medical illness.

Substance reaction, misuse and abuse

can cause out-of-control anger. Prescription medications taken as directed can have negative side-effects, sometimes including impulsivity and rage. Illicit or street drugs and alcohol can have similar effects, particularly when mixed. Medical attention is necessary any time substances are suspected to cause such negative outcomes.

Immaturity

Is how we all start. Dependent on others for all of our biological necessities, only gradually able to regulate the rhythms of our own bodies and modulate our own experience of emotion.

This infantile state remains at the foundation of who we become, the bedrock upon which all subsequent growth and learning are layered like floors in a skyscraper.

Stress (fatigue, hunger, illness and unexpected change) can cause regression, the elevator down from the highest level of maturity back toward the basement. Young children tend to regress into this infantile state more easily, but even the most sophisticated and mature adult can regress into an out-of-control, infantile state, given sufficient stress.

Immaturity is often unrelated to chronological age. Most dramatically, mental retardation and developmental delays including Asperger's Syndrome can cause individuals of any age to act in a relatively immature way, in some instances making out-of-control behavior more likely.

If we understand that mature functioning develops **through the process of internalization** (that is, taking inside you what you have experienced from the outside), then it's possible to see that the immature child has yet to build the internal psychological structures necessary for adequate self-control. This child needs consistent, predictable and unemotional containment from caregivers in order to learn to remain in control.

When caregivers respond to an immature child's anger with their own anger, threats, punishment or abuse, and/or, when a child's spontaneous rage elicits intimidation, abandonment or abuse, **psychological illness can develop.**

Psychological Illness

Born of some combination of genetics and environment, some people develop maladaptive or dysfunctional patterns for expressing their emotions which psychiatrists have categorized into types of psychological illnesses.

Each of these requires consultation with a psychological professional, including consideration of the value of psychotherapy with or without medication.

1. **Post-traumatic Stress Disorder** or PTSD is a condition which can result from exposure to extreme and/or repeated trauma, including abuse, war and natural disaster.

   PTSD is often characterized by storms of uncontrollable emotion, sometimes elicited by events which resemble the original trauma.

2. **Intermittent Explosive Disorder** characterizes an individual with otherwise unexplained bouts of extreme anger.

   Poorly understood in psychiatric research, this may be a facet of an undiagnosed neurological difference.

3. **Manic Depressive or Bipolar Disorder** is a biological illness causing individuals to experience dramatically shifting cycles of mood, from extreme depression to a state of euphoria known as mania.

   The manic individual is often impulsive, demanding and can become out-of-control.

4. **Psychosis** is the experience of misperceiving reality. It can include visual or auditory hallucinations or unfounded beliefs (called delusions) which are sometimes associated with out-of-control anger.

   Individuals can become psychotic as a result of a drug reaction or overdose, in the extremes of anxiety or depression or as part of a lifelong pattern illness called schizophrenia.

5. **Physical injury and medical illness** can be associated with out-of-control behavior.

   Head injuries, in particular, can impact personality and behavior in very serious ways. In addition, illnesses including diabetes, thyroid dysfunction and epilepsy can influence how an individual is able to express strong emotion.

What to do?

The formula for action is simple: The more violent, the more destructive and the longer-standing the problem, the more immediate and decisive the response must be.

A periodically out-of-control toddler may be very disruptive, but is more acceptable than a teenager who explodes into violence daily.

A third grader who lashes out at his friends impulsively and trashes his room when he tantrums is quite different than a young adult who is preoccupied with bombs and suicide.

As a general rule

Any threat to safety must be acted on promptly. Calling your local police department both helps to assure safety and communicates how serious the problem is to all involved.

Better to risk overreacting than to risk under-reacting.

The police can advise you about longer term solutions including court supervision of children who are out-of-control and can advise you about local resources that might be of help including anger management workshops.

Remember

1. Better to err on the side of safety. Call the police immediately if you believe that someone is in danger.

2. When out-of-control anger is associated with medication, illicit drugs or a suspected injury or illness, contact a physician first.

When out-of-control anger does not threaten safety, strategies such as those presented here can be useful.

A consistent team approach including the support of a mental health professional (psychologist, psychiatrist and/or social worker) and school (teachers, staff, administration) involvement will be critical.

Asking for outside help
Psychotherapy, medication and the courts

Better to err on the side of safety than to risk anyone's health and safety.

When anger is recurrent, explosive, violent or disruptive, when anger leads to escalating conflict, interferes with eating, sleeping, concentrating or doing your job as parent, spouse, employee, friend, child or student . . .

. . . it's time to ask for help.
But where?

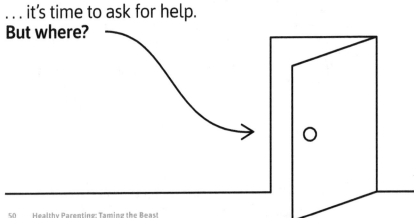

12

In this age of managed healthcare

your insurance benefits for medical and mental health care may be closely regulated.

Hard as it may be to ask for help, embarrassing as it may be talk through the details of the problem, if you want your insurance carrier to reimburse some or all of the costs involved, you may need to start with your primary care physician (PCP) or your child's pediatrician.

Some PCPs and pediatricians

are more likely to try to address the problem themselves. It is reasonable at this level to rule out obvious medical conditions which can be associated with anger expression (see Chapter 11) including thyroid dysfunction, blood sugar levels, head injury and—in some cases—epilepsy.

By starting off with a full physical examination including vision and hearing screenings, you can begin to clarify which of two primary paths to follow in further addressing the problem, the medical or the psychological.

Mental health services

vary dramatically by kind of provider and kind of service. Whether you search the internet, work from a list of managed care preferred providers or take the recommendations of family and friends, it is most important that you feel comfortable with and trust the mental health provider you choose.

There are many different kinds of mental health providers in as many different settings. In general:

1. **Pastoral counselors and clergy** will be available to you through houses of worship and affiliated centers.

   These providers are likely to bring a religious perspective to your concerns. Take the time with these as with any provider to inquire about training, experience and approach to matters of anger management.

2. **Schools and employers** often provide in-house or affiliated counselors (through an Employee Assistance Program or EAP, for example) with a variety of training, expertise and availability.

   In general, these providers can be especially useful to respond to an acute crisis, for short term help and as a referral source to other services. Costs for these services are often very low and subsidized by the school district or employer.

3. **Non-medical mental health professionals** include psychologists (with a Ph.D. or Psy.D. after their names), social workers (with an M.S.W., L.C.S.W., or C.C.S.W. after their names) and master's level clinicians (with an M.A. or M.S. after their names).

   The differences among these professionals are much more a matter of personality and approach than their specific degree or the initials after their names. It is not necessarily the case, for example, that a doctoral level provider (Ph.D. or Psy.D.) has more to offer than a master's level provider. (Nevertheless, you may find that managed health care companies discriminate by degree.)

4. **Medical mental health providers** are physicians (M.D.) or nurses (R.N.) with specific training in mental health care.

   Psychiatrists and neurologists, for example, are M.D.s who bring a medical or pharmacological (medicines) perspective to questions about anger management and quite different from a psychologist (Ph.D.) who is more likely to be concerned with behavior and relationships.

5. **Perspective, training and approach** vary across providers, regardless of degree or setting.

   The question here is about how you want to approach the problem? Some providers will want to explore the past in the hope of identifying events related to the present problem.

   These are often known as *analysts*. Others will think first in terms of drugs that may help change body and brain functioning. These are generally physicians and nurses. Still others will prefer to focus on making changes in behavior and thinking in the here-and-now. These are often called *behaviorists* or *cognitive-behaviorists*.

   This book takes a cognitive behavioral approach to anger management.

6. **Hospitals** used to admit children and adolescents with serious anger management problems easily and hold them for many weeks if not months.

   Financial restrictions have dramatically reduced such programs, even for the few who need such intensive psychological and medical treatments.

   Today, children, teens and adults are hospitalized as a last resort, particularly when there is a risk of imminent acts of violence (suicide or homicide) and then only briefly.

   Hospitalization is generally looked upon as an opportunity for stabilization, medication adjustment and launching back into (hopefully) a supportive network of family, therapists and educators.

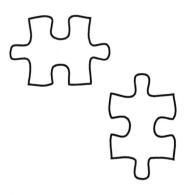

To medicate or not to medicate?

That is a thorny question, particularly given some providers' and managed care companies' emphasis on drug therapies. There are some situations which require medication (or other medical interventions) without question.

Anger problems related to thyroid dysfunction, for example, require medication. For those other, less certain situations, this book recommends a conservative approach, generally preferring behavioral strategies and advising against drug therapies whenever possible.

As a general rule, the need for drug therapies can be based on a combination of two measurements:

The individual's **subjective distress** and the individual's **objective dysfunction.**

---

1. **Subjective distress**

   Is measured from zero to 10, where zero means no distress and 10 corresponds to overwhelming, destructive internal emotional pain. As distress approaches ten, people tend to experience increasing worry, fear, anger and/or sadness, depending on the cause. Zero is unrealistic for most people, where the pressures of daily living routinely reach the level of 2 or 3 on this scale. Children can relate their internal upset or pain in the same way or, more concretely, by showing a relative distance between two hands. Beware that subjective distress is entirely subject to an individual's willingness to reveal what hurts inside. Some people will be more likely to under-report and others may be prone to over-report their distress.

2. **Objective dysfunction**

   Measures an individual's ability to fulfill their reasonable day-to-day responsibilities from the outside looking in. Is a parent taking reasonable care of her child? Is a spouse fulfilling his role toward his partner? Is a mature child, teen or adult caring for their own bodies, eating, dressing, sleeping and toileting as might be expected of their age? Is a student keeping up with class work, homework and grades? Is a child performing usual and reasonable chores? On a zero to 10 scale, zero means no dysfunction. At zero a person is completely fulfilling their responsibilities for their age, maturity level and circumstance. As dysfunction approaches 10, daily functioning breaks down. At 10, a person may be so completely disabled that she can't get out of bed, stops eating, bathing, caring for herself and others.

Which medications?

If medication is either your preferred intervention or may be necessary, get educated now.

Make an appointment to consult with your physician simply to learn more. Ask questions about types of medication, how they differ, possible side effects and all of your fears. Take the pharmacist aside at the local drug store and ask more.

Don't hesitate to get second and third opinions.
Consult the Internet, friends, family and professionals.

When to medicate?

Among the variables to consider is timing. Some medications have an immediate effect (stimulants like Ritalin®, for example) while others can take six to eight weeks before you see an effect (the SSRI anti-depressants, like Prozac®, for example).

If distress and dysfunction are worsening and the likely medication does not have an immediate impact, it's best to plan ahead.

Threshold events

Quite apart from medication decisions based on distress and dysfunction are decisions based upon circumstances. Certain *threshold events* may push toward medication sooner.

Fourth grade, for example, is just such a threshold event for kids. Anger management difficulties (disruptive, defiant, bullying or distracted behaviors, for example) will have less of an impact on educational achievement and peer relationships before fourth grade.

Curriculum changes and the typical solidification of the peer group among nine- and ten-year-olds make prompt resolution of difficulties that persist as fourth grade approaches more and more important.

Other threshold events might include a family's relocation, change of schools, beginning a new job, marriage and birth of a child.

The justice system

Calling the police strikes most parents as too extreme, no matter their spouse's or child's action. To some it suggests weakness, an inability to settle a problem unassisted and a breach of family privacy.

In fact, when strong emotion threatens anyone's health and safety, calling the police can be a necessary and life-saving step.

In general, the police and the courts do not want to interfere in your family's life. When called into the midst of a conflict, most police departments will do the minimum necessary to assure safety. When the aggressor is a child, once safety is ensured, most police officers will settle for a stern warning. When the problem persists, a child might be transported to the police station in an effort to convey the seriousness of the situation.

Aggressive older teens and adults may be subject to restraining orders and criminal prosecution in the extreme, steps aimed largely at assuring safety and punishing a serious offender. Neither is necessarily therapeutic. Both are generally short term measures.

When angry actions threaten family safety in the context of parental separation and divorce, lawyers and courts often examine visitation and custodial schedules. While such changes may relieve some of these difficulties, the relief is often short-lived. Child-centered professionals (child psychologists, for example) may still be necessary to advise the courts and/or to conduct therapies in pursuit of real change.

Finally, state child welfare or child protection agencies are often involved when children become violent or are victims of violence.

How these agencies operate varies depending on where you live, but the general rule is to disrupt families as little as possible. Even when a child must be removed from his home under extreme circumstances (an expensive and time-consuming commitment on the part of the state) the goal generally remains reunion with the family of origin.

13

If you only read one chapter, read this one

Okay, at least you're honest. You're not interested in reading chapter-by-chapter, wading through a lot of psychobabble and scary statements that will only prompt you to think, *"That'll never happen to me!"*

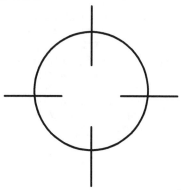

Here's the scoop, short and sweet.

Chapter references follow in parentheses, just in case you want to learn more.

1. It's okay to be mad. **(Chapter 2)**

2. Anger (and other strong emotion) that is not expressed can cause serious illness. **(Chapter 3)**

3. Some ways of showing anger are not okay.

4. It is your job as a parent to teach your kids how to show their anger acceptably. **(Chapter 4)**

5. The best way to teach your kids is by being a model of healthy anger expression yourself: Practice what you preach.

6. The flip side of the coin is also true: Expect your kids to do as you do, not as you say.

7. It is very useful to distinguish different degrees ("sizes") of anger. **(Chapter 5)**

8. It is even more useful to agree on the words that correspond to different sizes of anger. For example, is "frustrated" more or less than "irritated"? **(Chapter 6)**

9. Expect that no one thinks clearly when they're angry.

10. Plan ahead for what is okay to do when anger erupts. **(Chapter 7)**

11. Plan ahead for how to talk about an angry incident after it's over: Focus on making changes for the future. **(Chapter 8)**

12. Practice your anger management strategies every day. **(Chapter 10)**

13. Ask for help when anger becomes destructive or violent. **(Chapters 11 and 12)**

14. Be a well-informed consumer: Learn as much as you can about the different kinds of therapists, doctors, medications and community services available.

15. Teach healthy anger expression to others in your community.

Benjamin D. Garber, PhD is a New Hampshire licensed psychologist. He serves the needs of children whose parents are conflicted, separated and divorced as a child and family therapist, custody evaluator, parenting coordinator, expert witness and formerly as a Guardian ad litem. Dr. Garber provides advance training to family law professionals in all matters related to understanding and serving the needs of children. He is a prolific, award-winning author.

Dr. Garber's website is **www.healthyparent.com**

Other Books by

Benjamin D. Garber, PhD

Caught in the Middle (2019)

Holding Tight/Letting Go (2015)

The Roadmap to the Parenting Plan Worksheet (2015)

Ten Child-Centered Forensic Family Evaluation Tools (2015)

The Healthy Parent's ABCs (2015)

Developmental Psychology for Family Law Professionals (2009)

Keeping Kids Out of the Middle (2008)

Also in the **Healthy Parenting** series:

The Healthy Parent's ABCs
Benjamin Garber PhD

Twenty-six letters. Twenty-six lessons. Caregiving environments, schools and child-centered organizations assign one letter per week to complete the alphabet in full twice each year!

This fun little book is a simple "how to" guide for new parents. It is intended to be a quick and easy way to get professional parenting advice in small bites! *The Healthy Parent's ABCs* is parenting made simple. Laid out in twenty-six sections corresponding to the letters of the English alphabet, couples, groups or classes can move from one lesson to the next, one letter at a time. It's an entire curriculum for anyone!

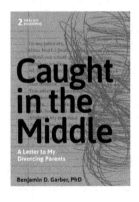

Caught in the Middle: A Letter to My Divorcing Parents
Benjamin Garber PhD

Do you worry that your relationship conflict is harming your children? Separation and divorce are tough enough on grown-ups, and they can be even tougher on kids. Parents may expect their children to be their allies, messengers, or spies. That's a lot of pressure for a kid! And it doesn't have to be this way.

In Caught in the Middle: A Letter to My Parents, Dr. Benjamin Garber shares Olivia's story of how parental conflict feels to a child. You'll learn practical strategies for cooperating, communicating, and putting your kids' needs first, so they can have the childhood they deserve.